P9-DFM-313

UNIVERSITIES IN TUDOR ENGLAND

DATE DUE

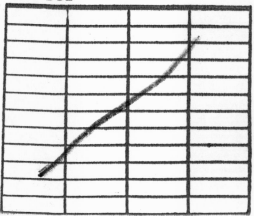

DEMCO

Universities
in
Tudor England

BY CRAIG R. THOMPSON

FOLGER BOOKS

Published by
THE FOLGER SHAKESPEARE LIBRARY

AN earlier booklet in this series described elementary and grammar-school training in Tudor England. The present essay attempts to sketch very briefly the organization and work of the two universities, Oxford and Cambridge. It is limited to those institutions as places of teaching and learning; it does not consider such interesting but extraneous topics as college architecture, which is better studied on the site.

Universities were a medieval product, a manifestation of intellectual activity in certain cities in the twelfth century. *Universitas*, a word meaning simply guild or corporation, came to be used of associations of scholars which had curricula, rules of government, recognition by some authority, and power to confer degrees. Oxford and Cambridge were formal associations of this kind. Essentially they were, and still are, corporations of Masters, Fellows, and Scholars engaged in teaching and learning the "arts" (including philosophy) and sciences. As corporations, early universities had two common forms, one typified by Bologna and the other represented by Paris and imitated by British and later by North American universities. Bologna, reputed the oldest university, was organized in the fashion often longed for by modern undergraduates: it was controlled by the students, who even hired and fired professors and prescribed their duties. Paris, on the other hand, was a guild of Masters of Arts, mature scholars who both taught and ruled the younger men.

Medieval university work was professional in aims. Most students were graduate students looking forward to careers in law, medicine, or theology. But since professional studies were not, as a rule, taken up until one became Bachelor of Arts, universities necessarily included undergraduates also. Members of a university had the status of "clerks," an important advantage because of the protection thus afforded against harassment by townsmen or petty officials. We should not conclude, however, that, because students were clerks or because theology as "queen of the sciences" dominated medieval intellectual life, university training was therefore mainly religious. There was little religion in the Arts curriculum. Nor should we suppose that, because of the prestige of theology, a deep sabbath of intellectual tranquillity reigned within the university. A medieval university was no ivory tower. Life in the thirteenth-century University of Paris was probably more turbulent than it is in any university today. Bitter ideological conflicts, with far-reaching consequences, raged within from time to time, while externally the University was often at odds with civil or ecclesiastical authority.

Long before the reign of Queen Elizabeth I, Oxford and Cambridge were venerable homes of learning. They had played a part in every chapter of the national religious and intellectual history since the close of the twelfth century. Like other national institutions, for example Parliament, their condition in 1500 or 1600 was due to accident as well as design, to unexpected and frequently unwelcome changes, to adaptations to new demands. Both universities remained largely medieval in curriculum and customs. Innovations did not always displace inheritances; new and old were adjusted in a manner practicable enough to serve the universities' purposes, flexible enough to respect ancient statutes and ceremonies. Elizabethan university conditions otherwise puzzling, or wholly unintelligible by academic standards or superstitions now prevalent, usually become more clear if examined from a medieval instead of a modern standpoint.

In 1500 Oxford and Cambridge each had ten colleges; by 1600 each had sixteen. At Oxford the oldest were University, Balliol, and Merton, all founded in the thirteenth century. Then came Exeter, Oriel, Queen's, and New College in the fourteenth century, and in the fifteenth Lincoln, All Souls, and Magdalen. The six Tudor colleges were founded between 1512 and 1571: Brasenose, Corpus Christi, Cardinal (afterward Christ Church),

Trinity, St. John's, Jesus. In addition to these colleges, Oxford in 1600 had at least eight halls or hostels: St. Edmund, Broadgates, Magdalen, St. Mary's, Hart, New Inn, St. Alban's, and Gloucester. These were survivors of dozens more that had existed at various times; there had been at least eight named Broadgates, nine named White. Some halls became absorbed by colleges; for example, a White Hall by Jesus College. In the reign of Charles I seven halls still existed; today only one, St. Edmund, remains.

Of Cambridge colleges the oldest was Peterhouse, founded in the thirteenth century. In the next century Clare, Pembroke, Gonville (since the Elizabethan reign called Gonville and Caius), Trinity Hall, and Corpus Christi (commonly called Bene't) were established; in the fifteenth, King's, Queens', St. Catharine's, and Jesus; in the sixteenth, between 1505 and 1596, Christ's, St. John's, Magdalene, Trinity, Emmanuel, and Sidney Sussex. As at Oxford, there had been other colleges and halls, but by 1600 these had disappeared or had been merged with new foundations or absorbed by them; Michaelhouse and King's Hall into Trinity, for example, and God's House into Christ's, Buckingham College into Magdalene. At least twenty sixteenth-century halls are known.

The corporate title of the universities was "The Chancellor, Masters, and Scholars of the University" of Oxford or Cambridge. Each university was a loosely federated republic of colleges. Each college had its own statutes and was governed by a head (Master, President, Provost, Warden, Dean, or Rector) and a body of Fellows. For the present we are more concerned with the university as a whole than with its component parts, for it was the university, not the colleges, that conferred degrees.

The highest dignitary was the Chancellor, elected for life by Masters and Doctors to this honorary, usually nonresidential, but powerful office. He presided on certain ceremonial occasions, intervened on the university's behalf with other influential personages when necessary, looked out for its interests at Court, and sometimes adjudicated internal disputes. His court exercised power, extending even to imprisonment, over all members of the university and over the city of Oxford or town of Cambridge, for the universities had jurisdiction over all local tradesmen.

Tudor Chancellors of Oxford and Cambridge were eminent ecclesiastics or statesmen, great men of affairs. Five of the sixteenth-century Chancellors of Cambridge, as Oxford historians like to point out, were beheaded for treason. One of these, Bishop John Fisher, dominated the University for thirty-five years. He served as Vice-Chancellor in 1501 and was Chancellor from 1504. He was President of Queens' College, 1505–1508, and helped to establish Christ's and St. John's. When his resistance to Henry VIII's ecclesiastical policies brought him to the block in 1535, he was succeeded in the chancellorship by the King's chief minister, Thomas Cromwell, who served until he too was executed (1540). Other Chancellors were Stephen Gardiner, Bishop of Winchester (1540–1547 and 1553–1555); the Duke of Somerset (1547–1552); the Duke of Northumberland (1552–1553); Cardinal Reginald Pole (1556–1558), who was also Chancellor of Oxford; William Cecil, Lord Burleigh (1559–1598); the Earl of Essex (1598–1601); and Sir Robert Cecil, Burleigh's son (1601–1612). Foremost of Elizabethan Chancellors of Oxford was the Earl of Leicester, who held office from 1564 until 1588. He was followed by Sir Christopher Hatton (1588–1591) and Thomas Sackville, Lord Buckhurst (1591–1608).

Presiding over the day-to-day business of the university and representing it in its manifold relations with Chancellor, bishops, and town was the Vice-Chancellor. Unlike post-Reformation Chancellors, he was a resident academician, thoroughly conversant with the university's customs and privileges, all of which it was his duty to maintain against menaces from whatever quarter. By custom the Chancellor nominated the Vice-Chancellor until Elizabethan times. Leicester experimented with election instead of appointment at Oxford in 1566 but was so displeased by the results that he took matters into his own hands again for a time. At Cambridge the Vice-Chancellor was elected

St. John Fisher, Bishop of Rochester (1469–1535),
the leading figure in Cambridge affairs in the early
part of the sixteenth century. He was Vice-Chancellor of the University in 1501, President of Queens'
College from 1505 to 1508, and Chancellor from
1504 until his death. (By an unknown sixteenth-
century artist, after Hans Holbein. Courtesy of the
National Portrait Gallery, London.)

William Cecil, Lord Burleigh (1520–1598), Lord Treasurer and Queen Elizabeth's chief minister; Chancellor of Cambridge from 1559 to 1598. (Engraving by an unknown artist.)

by heads of colleges after 1570, and after 1586 every holder of the office was himself head of a college.

Next in importance to Chancellor and Vice-Chancellor were the proctors, elected annually. They had the duty of enforcing university discipline and regulations for town and gown. Because they were also in charge of academic ceremonies and protocol of all kinds, they played a large role in the daily life of the university. Each university had likewise a "high steward," a nonresident officer with certain legal duties. Thomas More served for a few years as steward of both universities. Esquire bedells (whose functions included that of escorting professors to lecture halls and students to degree-taking ceremonies), sub-proctors, clerks, registrars, and other minor officials need not detain us.

The legislature of each university consisted of its Masters, "regent" and "non-regent," and Doctors. Regents were men who, having lately become M.A., now devoted some time to teaching and to presiding at disputations. In Elizabethan Oxford one's period of regency lasted one or two years; at Cambridge, after 1570, five years.

Oxford had two legislative houses or assemblies, Congregation and Convocation. Congregation, the smaller, was composed of Regent Masters and of Doctors, though Doctors usually left the business to the Masters. Congregation controlled and supervised the routine of lectures and disputations; therefore it controlled the requirements for degrees. Convocation, the more powerful body, included all Non-Regents as well as Regents. At times it delegated powers to Congregation—for example, power to act on requests from students of all grades for dispensations from required periods of residence—but reserved supreme authority for itself. Also it elected the Chancellor and proctors.

Cambridge government in Elizabethan times was vested in a Senate made up of two houses of Regents and Non-Regents. There was also a Caput Senatus, a council consisting of the Vice-Chancellor and five other members, usually heads of houses. Until 1570 the Caput was appointed at the start of each

Robert Dudley, Earl of Leicester (1532–1588),
High Steward of Cambridge University, 1562, and
Chancellor of Oxford from 1564 to 1588. (Engraving by Willem van de Passe.)

session of the two houses; after 1570, for a year. The Caput became a sort of executive committee. It decided, for instance, whether "graces" (proposals or motions) might be submitted to the Senate.

Westminster and Canterbury kept a close eye on the universities and had many methods, direct and indirect, of making their power felt. This influence was natural, inevitable, in a society in which Church and State were so intimately connected. At the commencement of a new reign it was imperative for the universities to secure a renewal of their rights and privileges. From time to time their fundamental statutes were revised, or new ones imposed, by the Government, ordinarily after investigation of university affairs by a royal commission. This happened, for example, after the death of Henry VIII, when a Government more decisively Protestant came into power. Bishop Gardiner, who was hostile to Reformed doctrine, was replaced as Chancellor of Cambridge by Protector Somerset. A royal commission with broad powers inspected Oxford and Cambridge and afterward issued new statutes. These revised the curriculum and the rules for election of university officers, student dress, worship, and many other matters. In Mary Tudor's reign (1553–1558) England again became officially Roman Catholic. Administrators and candidates for degrees were now required to affirm their Catholicism and acceptance of papal supremacy. Cardinal Pole, Archbishop of Canterbury and Chancellor of both universities, appointed a new commission for university reform. Statutes of Edward's reign were rescinded and new ones, revising university government, were substituted. Since these Marian statutes did not last long enough to make much difference, they do not need description here.

Early in Elizabeth's reign the Edwardian statutes, with slight changes, were reinstituted. A new reign, a new commission: this time to undo the Romanizing of the preceding one. The Edwardian statutes as now restored prevailed at Cambridge until 1570, at Oxford until Archbishop Laud's were issued in 1634–1636. In 1570 Cambridge received another and definitive set of statutes. These purported to improve university organization but in reality were intended just as much to curb the strength and factiousness of young Fellows of colleges, some of whom had strong Puritan sympathies. Ever since 1559 the younger M.A.'s had been the most powerful single group in the University. The statutes of 1570, drawn up by John Whitgift, Master of Trinity, and his friends and clearly based on the Edwardian ones, were approved by Cecil and imposed on the University, despite vigorous protest from many of the Fellows. These new statutes gave effectual control of the University to the heads of colleges, who alone could nominate men for the office of Vice-Chancellor. The Vice-Chancellor's power to imprison members of the University was increased. The Caput was henceforth to be elected by heads and Doctors and to serve for a year at a time. Within each college the Master was to have a veto at all elections of Fellows. To crown Whitgift's victory, he himself was chosen Vice-Chancellor in 1570.

Only the university awarded degrees, but a person had to be admitted to a college before he could become a member of the university. Each college set its own standards for entrance, but all had certain requirements in common. Obviously a freshman had to be competent in Latin, since most lectures and virtually all textbooks were in that language. Every boy who completed grammar school had worked at Latin for seven years and for three or more had studied rhetoric. In addition to Latin, students from the better schools had had a good introduction to Greek. The elements of Christian doctrine, a little history, and less mathematics made up the rest of their school work.

A university's character is determined first of all by its purposes. The Privy Council, in a letter to Cambridge, 1575, affirmed these to be liberal education and the professional study of divinity: the universities "have at the first been instituted principally for the nurture and education of a multitude of youth in good manners, learning, and Christianity, and likewise for the maintenance and sustenation of such as should there teach all liberal sciences and exercise the study and profession of divinity." Going to a university was not then the "thing to do" for everybody who could afford it. Most of those who went had definite professional ambitions in law, medicine, or theology. Not all students took or sought degrees, however. For some it was the residence, not the degree, that mattered. Others were not eligible for degrees and did not matriculate, for they wished to avoid subscribing to the Thirty-Nine Articles of the Church of England. Matriculation, formal registration in the university, was not required at Cambridge until 1544, at Oxford until 1565; admission to a college sufficed.

Universities granted Bachelors', Masters', and Doctors' degrees. Undergraduate studies ended, as they do now, with the B.A. degree. Men with a B.A. degree usually took an M.A. also before proceeding to professional studies, but it was possible to take a law or medical degree without taking an M.A. or even a B.A. degree. To become M.A. was the most important single achievement in academic life. Not only was this degree the most common gateway to professional degrees but by custom it entitled the holder to the *ius docendi ubique:* the right, recognized by the entire academic world, to teach or lecture anywhere. He could instruct undergraduates and preside at disputations, and he could claim a share in the government of the university.

The traditional faculties were Arts, Law, Medicine, and Theology. Men who stayed the full course and met all statutory requirements for a professional degree were in residence for many years. The requirement for an M.A. degree was three years of study beyond the four needed for B.A.; for a Bachelor of Divinity degree, seven additional years beyond the M.A.; for a doctorate in Divinity (then an earned degree, not a gift), four or five years beyond the B.D. Thus a D.D. could take a man almost twenty years, though it must be added at once that residence requirements for advanced degrees beyond M.A. were very often modified or waived. Statutes may have been explicit, but generosity in granting dispensations became habitual. Illness, clerical duties, other studies, travel, schoolmastering, and a hundred other of the usual excuses enabled many men to proceed M.A. or B.D. in much less than the statutory period. Cambridge's new statutes of 1570 endeavored to correct this abuse by forbidding dispensations that permitted a man to omit some exercises or shorten his period of residence, but sabotage by University officers partially thwarted this decree. Oxford too, in the 1570's, made a half-hearted attempt to reduce the number of dispensations.

The Elizabethan Arts course was based firmly on the old medieval *trivium* and *quadrivium*. In his first two years an undergraduate studied mostly rhetoric and Aristotelian logic and some arithmetic and music. In his second year or at the end of it he was admitted to disputations, and in his third and fourth years he had to engage in two of these in his college and two in public. His disputations, lectures, and exercises in the third and fourth years were devoted to the "three philosophies" of Aristotle. Although undeniably conservative, the Arts course did not escape occasional review and adjustment. Royal injunctions of 1535 ordained that students be instructed in logic, rhetoric, arithmetic, music, geography, and philosophy. A royal commission of 1549, however, ruled that the first undergraduate year at both universities should consist of mathematics and that grammar had to be completed before one came to the university. The second year was to be given to logic, the third and fourth to philosophy. How much mathematics the Arts student learned we do not know; certainly it was nothing very advanced. The "mathematicals," as they were called, may have included elements of astronomy, but on the whole we hear little about mathematics in contemporary descriptions of universities.

The ordinances of 1549 were hardly affected by visitorial commissions of the next dozen years, with the important exception that grammar and rhetoric were restored to the freshman year. Cambridge statutes of 1570 contemplate rhetoric in the first year, logic in the second and third, philosophy in the fourth, in addition to participation in two college disputations and two in the "Schools" (the university lecture and disputation halls).

The end and rationale of these studies are obvious. They aimed at an intellectual discipline based on rhetoric and philosophy. One began by mastering the tools of learning, working from simple to complex: first the grammar of language, then its uses as an instrument of thought (logic) and communication or discourse (rhetoric, which included poetry). The logic studied included the predicables, categories, concepts of judgment, deductive and inductive reasoning, and fallacies. A "new" type of logic, that of Peter Ramus (1515–1572), had a vogue for a time, largely because of its supposedly bold independence of Aristotle's and its attractiveness as a short cut to mastery of the subject. The *Dialectica* of Ramus became a popular textbook, especially at Cambridge. For the philosophical studies of the third and fourth years, Aristotle's scientific writings and his *Metaphysics, Ethics,* and *Politics* supplied the fundamental texts. Inasmuch as Aristotle's thought was the basis of medieval Scholastic philosophy, we might have expected him to share the disfavor shown to medieval philosophers after the Reformation. Not at all. On many subjects he was still "the master of them that know" in the Tudor curriculum. The old formula for taking the B.A. degree, requesting permission to "read [lecture on] a book of Aristotle's logic," was still in use and still relevant.

Some history and geography found their way into the B.A. course, but the main fare in the sixteenth and seventeenth centuries continued to be grammar and rhetoric, logic and philosophy. Modern languages were studied by some, but these were extracurricular subjects. Greek was the only significant addition to the Arts curriculum in the sixteenth century; in fact Greek was the hallmark of progress in the academic world of the earlier Tudors. To some minds its attractions were literary and philosophical; to others its importance lay in its unique contribution to theological studies and Biblical criticism. Greek was scarcely studied in medieval England. Not until the late fifteenth century did it appear as an interest at Oxford, where for many years it had only a handful of students. During the reign of Henry VIII, Greek became securely established as an academic discipline. Statutes of new colleges provided for it; older colleges added it. Thus Corpus Christi, Oxford, founded in 1515 by a former Chancellor of Cambridge, had from the beginning a lecturer in Greek whose duty it was to discourse daily on Greek grammar, rhetoric, and literature. Lectureships in Greek

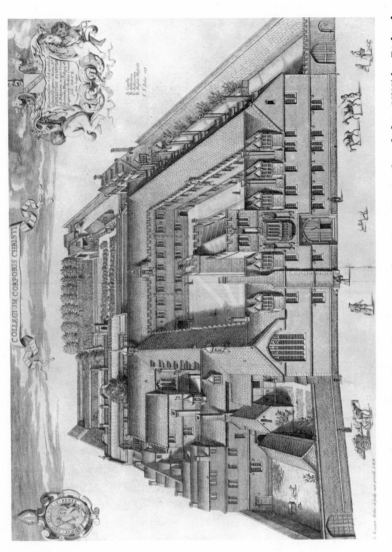

Corpus Christi College, Oxford, in the seventeenth century. It was founded in 1515 by Richard Foxe, Bishop of Winchester, whose statutes provided for public Readers in Latin, Greek, and Divinity. (From David Loggan, *Oxonia Illustrata*, 1675.)

are said to have been set up at Magdalen, Merton, and Queen's in 1535, and in Greek and Latin at New College and All Souls; students from other colleges also were to attend the lectures. Cambridge's distinctive tradition of Greek scholarship begins with Erasmus, who was invited to the university by Fisher and lived and worked at Queens' College for several years (1511–1514). The royal injunctions of 1535, issued when Thomas Cromwell was both Vicar-General of the realm and Chancellor of Cambridge, ordered every college there to have two daily public lectures on Greek and Latin. But this scheme does not seem to have been carried out at that time in more than a few colleges. St. John's, founded in 1511, was the home of some of the century's best Hellenists: Richard Croke, Sir John Cheke, and Roger Ascham.

We may conclude, then, that the B.A. course in the sixteenth century was mainly traditional, medieval, in content. Academic humanism, best symbolized perhaps by cultivation of Greek and, after 1535, rejection of Scotus, Aquinas, and others of that ilk, broadened the intellectual range of English universities, bringing their studies closer to what later generations would consider a "liberal" education. Within thirty years, wrote Erasmus in 1517, Cambridge had changed from a place where nothing was heard but Scholastic logic, Aristotle, and Scotus to one where literature, mathematics, "a new or at least renovated Aristotle," and Greek now existed. Yet, however much tone and tastes shifted during the century, the formal Arts curriculum changed relatively little. This fact is not surprising nor is it inconsistent with Erasmus' statement, for the most effective or significant intellectual activity in a university is not necessarily visible in the round of studies for the B.A.

Taking the degree at the end of the four-year course involved an elaborate ritual, substantially the same in both universities. At Elizabethan Oxford a student, after first securing permission from his college, "supplicated" or formally asked Congregation for leave to proceed to a degree. Accompanied by a Regent Master of his college, he went to St. Mary's, the University church, where the Regent presented his "supplicat" to Congregation, which voted on it secretly. If the votes were favorable in four successive meetings of Congregation, the candidate received a "grace" or permission to be presented for a degree. On the day preceding his presentation he went through the motions of paying a call on senior officers of the University. After 1580 he subscribed to the Thirty-Nine Articles and took the oath of assent to the Royal Supremacy on degree day. Then the Vice-Chancellor conferred the degree of B.A. upon him. But even now he was not a full-fledged B.A. until he had engaged in certain climactic disputations called "Determinations." This was the arduous part of becoming Bachelor, for he had to stand against all comers who chose to oppose him on logical or philosophical questions; and this he had to do during most of the days of Lent. Similarly at Cambridge, where a student on completing the Arts course was examined by the proctors and Regent Masters and, after this formality, could present his "supplicat" to the Vice-Chancellor and Senate. Now a "questionist," he was interrogated briefly at a ceremony, and after "responding" was ready to "determine."

For an M.A. degree the statutory requirement was still three years of resident graduate study, but this standard was compromised by the universities' liberality in granting dispensations. In the Jacobean reign Cambridge abolished the residence requirement altogether, thus almost inevitably opening the way for the M.A. degree to degenerate to the purely formal one of today, which an Oxford or Cambridge graduate receives simply by staying alive for a stated number of years, keeping his name on the books, and paying a fee. If he had not obtained dispensations, an Oxford or Cambridge B.A. in Tudor times devoted three years to the "three philosophies" as preparation for the M.A. degree. He heard lectures on Aristotle's metaphysics, natural philosophy (physics), and moral philosophy, subjects to which he had been introduced as an undergraduate. He attended disputations regularly, taking part in one or two each year, and gave a few perfunctory lectures on set books. These studies made up the *quadrivium* of arithmetic, geometry, music, and astronomy, or rather had become the recognized substitute for it.

The procedure in taking the M.A. degree was much like that already described for the B.A.: the candidate obtained permission to proceed, "supplicated," and was presented to the Vice-Chancellor, who licensed him to lecture and dispute. He did not actually become M.A. until a year later, after having "incepted" (at Oxford) or "commenced" (at Cambridge). Inception or commencement, which took place in July, meant taking part in certain philosophical disputations called the "Vesperies" and the "Comitia" or "Act"; "act" being a generic term for a thesis defended in disputation. These too were elaborate, traditional ceremonies, though even from these the universities often granted dispensations. Now, if he continued at the university, he became a Regent Master and shared the work of instruction for a few years. After regency he joined one of the higher faculties, Law, Medicine, or Theology.

Except at Paris, law was probably the most popular of professional studies in Continental universities. In Elizabethan Oxford and Cambridge it was less popular than theology, not because the English were less litigious but because of the peculiar organization of legal studies in England and the effects of the Reformation on one important branch of law there. Common law was the province of the Inns of Court in London, not of the universities, which restricted themselves to canon (ecclesiastical) and civil (Roman) law. When the Government abolished the papal prerogative in England and eliminated at a stroke all the vast body of statutes and interpretations so long used in ecclesiastical courts, canon law became a stumbling block and irrelevancy and was accordingly banned. Fellowships for its study were gradually reassigned to students of civil law. The statutes of 1549 fostered civil law as emphatically as they denigrated canon law, but not so effectively. Only eight Cantabrigians became Bachelors of Civil Law between 1544 and 1551, only one Doctor of Laws. The subject had been ruined academically by divorce from canon law. Most political and legal questions raised by the Reformation in England were settled on the basis of common, not civil, law.

An Oxford M.A. seeking to become B.C.L. was supposed to study law for three years. But it was possible to enter the Faculty of Law directly after matriculation, avoiding the B.A. degree entirely. If a man did this, he could get a law degree in four or five years by attending lectures and engaging in disputations. A Cambridge man needed four years beyond the M.A. for a B.C.L. degree; without a B.A. he needed six years in all. By statute an Oxford candidate for the D.C.L. had to be a B.C.L. who had heard lectures for four or five years more before supplicating for the higher degree; but this requirement was frequently dispensed. A Cambridge B.C.L. was expected to study five more years; an M.A., seven more.

Medical education, like legal education, could be obtained at Tudor Oxford and Cambridge, but for prospective physicians or surgeons it became customary to go abroad, to Padua, Montpellier, or elsewhere, for professional training. Moralists might shudder at the dangers of foreign residence to English virtue, but the fact remained that medical education was more advanced on the Continent than in England. In medieval times the study was a medley of traditional remedies, ancient texts (Aristotle, Hippocrates, Galen), and astrology. Anatomy and dissection were uncommon, though not unknown; surgery was considered an inferior branch of the art. Most but not all medical students at Oxford went through the Arts course first. Cambridge allowed no alternative. At the end of eight years' study after matriculation, or four after the M.A. (five at Cambridge), they took the degree of Bachelor of Medicine and could then practice in Oxford or Cambridge. Two years of further study after the M.B. led to an M.D. degree. When we turn from the fourteenth to the sixteenth century, we find that medical students, according to the statutes of 1549, were to view two anatomies in addition to studying for six years and disputing twice before they could become M.B. They were to perform two anatomies and cure three patients before being admitted to surgical practice. For M.D. degrees they had to view two or three more anatomies, hear lectures, dispute, and have been M.B. for four or five years. Besides the degrees of M.B. and M.D., the universities granted licenses to practice surgery anywhere in England. The precise relation between licenses and degrees is not clear. Some Oxford men who supplicated for the license had already been practicing, while others supplicated for the license and the M.B. degree at the same time.

Gonville College, Cambridge, refounded in 1557 by Dr. John Caius, a distinguished physician who had studied with Vesalius in Padua, became a notable home of intending physicians. Two of the three fellowships Caius established were for medicine. Appropriately enough, this was the college of William Harvey, discoverer of the circulation of the blood. After taking his B.A. in 1597, Harvey, like Dr. Caius before him, went to Padua for medical study. Cambridge graduated a total of only thirty-two M.B.'s and M.D.'s between 1570 and 1590, but the number tripled between 1610 and 1640. Some of the topics of medical disputations in Elizabethan and Jacobean universities survive. Here are a few medical problems thought suitable for academic debate: "Whether life can be prolonged by the aid of the medical art" (a real question in those days); "Whether it is better to drink French or red wine than white with meals"; "Whether the frequent drinking of nicotine, commonly called tobacco, conduces to health"; "Whether a man can live more than seven days without food or drink" (did nobody try it?); and that old favorite, now handed over to the psychiatrists, "Whether love is a disease."

Of another degree, that in music, it need only be said that although the Elizabethan age was one of the great periods in English musical history, when the art was universally popular, music attracted very few followers as an academic pursuit. It received no attention in the statutes of 1549. Only about twenty-five men took degrees in music at Oxford between 1583 and 1610. To become Bachelor of Music there one was expected to study music for seven years and to compose and have performed a composition of five parts, described as a "choral hymn." To

19

become Doctor of Music a candidate had to be B. Mus. for five years and compose a song of six or eight parts. Boethius' *De Musica* was still a textbook, and the formula for the degree permitted the candidate to "lecture on some book by Boethius on music."

Supreme among advanced degrees was Theology, and next to Arts it had also the largest number of candidates. In most of the older colleges the Arts course was intended to lead to Theology. Even in sixteenth-century foundations, for example Christ's, Cambridge, and Jesus, Oxford, the Arts course was regarded simply as a steppingstone toward Theology. A B.D. or D.D. degree, as we have learned, exacted long years of study. It presupposed Greek. It required attendance at lectures on the Bible, theology, and Hebrew; engagement in disputations; preaching. The royal injunctions of 1535 had dismissed Peter Lombard, Duns Scotus, and other standard medieval theologians from the curriculum, supplanting them with later authors more acceptable to the new ecclesiastical policies. Statutes of 1549 ordain that B.D.'s shall attend a theological lecture daily, dispute, and preach an English and a Latin sermon in the university church. This Latin sermon, known as the "clerum" because addressed to resident divines, became a public event attended by undergraduates and graduates alike. The clerum was only one of many sermons an undergraduate heard during the year. He was expected to attend university service on Sunday and college chapel on other days of the week. He had no formal courses in religion but was likely to receive informal instruction, in his college, on the Catechism. Theology was inescapable in a Tudor university.

The definitive Cambridge statutes of 1570 require that the M.A. be a "diligent hearer" of daily lectures on theology and Hebrew for seven years (five years sufficed at Oxford, apparently). He is to dispute twice against a B.D. and, after his fourth year, to "respond in Theology." He must preach an English and a Latin sermon in the University church and, within a year after incepting as B.D., preach at Paul's Cross in London. To become D.D. he is expected to study five years more (four at Oxford)

Christ's College, Cambridge. Founded in 1505 by Margaret Beaufort, Countess of Richmond, mother of King Henry VII. (From David Loggan, *Cantabrigia Illustrata*, 1676–1690.)

according to statute, to dispute, and to preach. In practice this period was very often shortened by dispensation. Some men even received permission to take B.D. and D.D. degrees together, but none could become D.D. without being B.D. The university licensed men to preach anywhere in England. Such a license was independent of a degree and had to be sought separately from it at some stage of the theologian's career; this meant, at Oxford at any rate, after he was M.A. and had preached within the university four times. In the Elizabethan Church no man could preach without a license from university or episcopal authority.

Throughout Elizabeth's reign the universities had difficulties with "popish recusants." Parliament strengthened the Act of Supremacy in 1563, making a second refusal to take the oath punishable as high treason, which meant by death. Papists were subsequently excluded from university degrees, and they remained excluded, as did other dissenters, until 1871. Roman Catholicism did not disappear at once but lingered on here and there in the universities until the 1570's. As late as 1572 the venerable Master of Gonville, Dr. Caius, was accused by his own Fellows of being secretly a practicing papist. His rooms were searched and the vestments and ornaments found there were publicly burned in the college court. Resentment against a papal bull (1570) excommunicating Elizabeth and absolving her subjects from their allegiance, the St. Bartholomew Massacre (1572), the menace of Mary Queen of Scots, and fears of Jesuit plots caused Parliament to pass a series of repressive measures against Catholics between 1571 and 1593. Some university scholars went into exile, as Protestant ones had done under Mary. Legal restrictions on Roman Catholics finally became so severe that no one at a university could openly proclaim sympathy with "popery" without risking serious trouble.

In some respects Puritanism presented a more obstinate problem than Romanism, since the issue between Anglicanism and Romanism seemed clear-cut, whereas Puritans were in the Church of England. They included members of all social classes, commanded the sympathies of many leading scholars in the universities, and had powerful support in Parliament. The intellectual energy of Puritanism, its emphasis on the Bible, hostility to ceremonialism, and, in its more radical adherents, preference for presbyterian over episcopal government were matters that could not fail to agitate the universities. For Oxford and Cambridge were not merely microcosms where debates echoed what went on in the larger world beyond college walls. They supplied that world with ideas and men; they were testing grounds where orthodoxy and dissent met in conflict, where election of a college head or a Fellow might indicate a definite shift in Puritan or anti-Puritan strength.

Academic warfare over Puritanism reached its first climax in 1570 at Cambridge, after a controversy led on the Puritan side by Thomas Cartwright, Fellow of Trinity. His opponent was Whitgift, the Master of Trinity and Regius Professor of Divinity. Whitgift had Cartwright deprived of his academic posts in 1570 and 1571. This affair became a *cause célèbre* in the Church and University. It began an interminable war of words, did much to make Puritanism a concern to Parliament, and finally helped to make Whitgift a bishop and afterward Archbishop of Canterbury. From Canterbury (1583–1604) he opposed Puritans as forcefully as he had done at Cambridge.

Cambridge remained the intellectual center of English Puritanism and of English Protestantism generally in the Tudor and Stuart reigns. This is not to say that Oxford slumbered in conformity and conservatism. It had more Catholics than Cambridge, or at least a reputation for more, but was swept by the same pattern of controversies as Cambridge. Its members read the same books and debated the same questions. Each university had first Catholic and then Puritan recusants and every variety of Anglican. But with two or three exceptions the great names of the Puritan movement were those of Cambridge men. Cecil, who as Chancellor of the University and chief minister of the Crown had power beyond which there was no appeal, found himself compelled to intervene repeatedly in order to mollify or discipline the more refractory brethren. He wrote somewhat testily in 1572 that he preferred to use his authority "for the benefit and preferment of the University than to bestow that little leisure I have from greater affairs in the compounding of your quarrels," but to the end of his life (1598) he heard complaints from and concerning Cambridge.

After this glance at the ecclesiastical setting we may return to university routine. Something must be said about methods of instruction. In medieval universities the teaching consisted of lectures by Regent Masters, each new M.A. being called upon in turn to do his share of the work. In Tudor Oxford and Cambridge the Regents still did much of the teaching, but there were now university professors and college tutors besides. This supplementing of university teaching by collegiate instruction was the most significant and lasting educational development in the Tudor universities. It suited the college system and proved more efficient than university teaching alone. College lectures, given in hall or chapel by lecturers appointed by the college, supplied the undergraduate with topics, arguments, and syllogisms he could use both in college and university disputations. These private lectures did not have the prestige of university ones but were perhaps more useful for that very reason, since they could supplement or continue the other kind or cover the same ground more thoroughly.

Public or university lectures were given by a professor in each faculty. No professorships had more honor than those established by Tudor royalty. Lady Margaret Beaufort, mother of Henry VII, founded with Fisher's advice the Lady Margaret Professorships of Divinity in each university (1502, 1503). Professors on this foundation were to lecture an hour per day on each weekday. Henry VIII founded and endowed Regius Professorships of Divinity, Civil Law, Medicine, Greek, and Hebrew (at Cambridge in 1540, at Oxford in 1546), a benefaction that aroused much enthusiasm. Cambridge statutes of 1570, which in this respect resemble those of 1549, ordain that University lecturers are to lecture four times a week. Theological lectures may deal only with Sacred Scripture. The law lecturer is to take up Roman civil law or the laws of the Anglican Establishment "and no other." In philosophy the lecturer is to discourse on Aristotle's physical, moral, and political works, Pliny *(Natural History)*, or Plato. Lecturers on medicine must expound Hippocrates or Galen. The lecturer on mathematics may explain cosmography by reference to Mela, Pliny, Strabo, or Plato (the curriculum ignores Columbus and Copernicus); arithmetic by works of two modern writers, Tunstall (late Bishop of Durham) or Cardanus; geometry by Euclid; astronomy by Ptolemy. For dialectics Aristotle's *Sophistical Questions* and Cicero's *Topics* are prescribed. For rhetoric the authors are Quintilian, Hermogenes, and Cicero; but these, it is added, are to be expounded in English, so the hearers will understand them. The Professor of Greek must choose Homer, Isocrates, Demosthenes, Euripides, or some other author. His colleague in Hebrew may lecture on no text but the Old Testament; also he is to teach the Hebrew language.

Lectures were "ordinary" and "extraordinary" or "cursory." Ordinary lectures, the more important kind, were formal expositions of particular topics or questions. A cursory lecture consisted of reading through a book and translating it, with comments. B.A.'s studying for M.A. degrees often gave cursory lectures. Ordinary lectures were delivered in the morning, cursory ones in the afternoon. As we have just noticed, a few Cambridge lectures were given in English. Most continued to be given in Latin. Going to a lecture was a serious affair, much more formal than it is now. Scholars escorted the lecturer to the hall. Attendance was compulsory at all lectures in one's faculty and fines were levied for missing them. Students "cut" them nevertheless, and in their ingenuity at thinking up excuses had little to learn from modern undergraduates. Lectures were commonly scheduled at seven or eight in the morning. A course of logic lectures founded at Cambridge in 1611 was to be offered from six to eight and the first hour of each lecture devoted to review and discussion of the previous day's discourse. Before this date we seldom hear of any discussion accompanying lectures. Auditors were expected to take notes.

Equally ancient and honored in university work, but entirely different from lectures in aims and methods, were the disputations. A legacy from medieval Scholasticism, formal disputation survived long after the introduction of printed textbooks and was still the principal mode of academic exercise in Spenser's and Milton's university days, still essentially Scholastic in character, purpose, and often in the very questions debated. If it did little to advance knowledge, it must at least have done much to sharpen wits. As a test of knowledge of logic and of skill in debate, and incidentally of Latin, it could be a crucial demonstration of a man's abilities. It served therefore as a sort of examination, for medieval and Tudor universities had no written tests.

After his second year each student took part in a stated number of disputations in college and in public. He engaged twice as "respondent" (a word recalled by the term still used for the Oxford entrance examination, "Responsions"), twice as "opponent," and his adversaries might be his contemporaries or older students. At Oxford—and Cambridge practice was more or less the same—his first disputation concerned grammatical or logical questions. Three such questions were debated at a disputation, one student acting as respondent and two others as opponents. A Regent Master presided and made an introductory speech. The respondent, who probably spoke first, then defended the affirmative side of the question; his opponents took the negative. Disputations for undergraduates in their third or fourth year and for B.A.'s dealt with philosophical questions, those for more advanced students with topics relevant to their professional faculties.

A man's friends attended his disputations and doubtless tried to encourage him as much as decorum allowed. Each disputant gave arguments, cross-examined the other speaker or speakers, and attempted to refute them, always attacking or defending by means of syllogisms and indeed by any other weapons of logic which he could lay hands on. Much solemn ritual, and some not so solemn, governed these displays. Public and private records preserve a large number of sixteenth- and seventeenth-century questions disputed at Oxford and Cambridge. As we may judge by the following examples from Oxford disputations for the

M.A., many would look quite familiar if we turned them freely into modern idiom. "An ex optimo academico fiat optimus aulicus" (1592) is the ancestor of countless freshman themes on whether a college education will get you ahead in politics. Or how hackneyed seems "An metropolis sit opportunior sedes academiis constituendis quam ignobilius oppidum" (1594): is it better for a university to be in a large city than in a one-horse town? Typical questions for dispute in the Arts faculty at Oxford included: whether the sea is salt (1576), whether women should have a liberal education (1581), whether a comet is helpful or harmful (1584), whether there are more worlds than one (1588), whether there is any certain knowledge of things (1595). At Cambridge in 1597 students in the Faculty of Civil Law debated the proposition: "Despite the judgment of scholars, the power of the sword is the prince's alone." In Theology we find: "The statecraft of Moses should not be binding on Christian commonwealths"; in Philosophy: "All change in the commonwealth is dangerous" and "The senses are not deceived." In all disputations, whatever the questions at issue, skill in argument was what mattered most. Rhetorical resourcefulness, cogency, the tactics of logic and eloquence combined: these carried the day.

The medieval colleges of Oxford and Cambridge had small libraries of chained books, some of which were still chained long after the Elizabethan period. Merton had the oldest college library in England. Oxford had a collection of manuscripts kept in St. Mary's Church, but it did not have a university library until Bishop Cobham of Worcester, in the fourteenth century, built a two-story House of Congregation, the first strictly university building at Oxford. The library occupied the second story. In the fifteenth century the Cobham library was replaced by a new one. This too was in the upper story of a new building, the Divinity School. The new library was a memorial to a great benefactor, Duke Humphrey of Gloucester, a collector who first gave manuscripts to the University in 1435 and continued to do so until his death in 1447.

The foundation of a new library at Oxford by Sir Thomas

Sir Thomas Bodley (1545–1613), founder of the Bodleian Library, Oxford. He was educated abroad and at Magdalen College and was a university lecturer before entering the Queen's service. From 1589 to 1596 he was her representative in the Netherlands. (Courtesy of the Bodleian Library, Oxford.)

Bodley (1545–1613), a diplomat and scholar, may well have been the most important event in the University's Tudor epoch. Bodley began in 1598 by restoring the old Duke Humphrey Library. He built an addition in 1610 and provided in his will for further enlargements. He gave his books to the University and persuaded other persons of means to contribute. He was one of the first of that most useful class of beggars, rich graduates who not only support alma mater generously but solicit others to do likewise and thus make charity fashionable. Use of the library was limited to Doctors, Masters, and Bachelors, but Bachelors had to get permission from Congregation. Bodley wanted no ephemeral productions cluttering up his library. Shakespeare's name does not appear in a Bodleian catalogue until 1635. But by an agreement Bodley fortunately made with the Stationers' Company, which controlled publishing and copyright, the library was entitled to receive on demand a copy of every book printed in England. By Act of Parliament in 1665 Cambridge's library began to share the same privilege.

The Cambridge library dates from ca. 1415 or earlier. The first catalogue listed fifty-two volumes; the second (1473) contained 330. As at Oxford, college libraries grew independently of the University library. Their treasures would take too long to describe, but the incomparable collection of historical manuscripts gathered by Archbishop Parker and given by him to Corpus Christi must not go unmentioned.

At first Oxford and Cambridge had no colleges; students lived wherever they could find lodgings. In time some lodging houses became the halls or hostels so often named in medieval or early Tudor accounts. A hall owned or hired by a Master and occupied by students easily acquired some of the characteristic marks of a college. Finally the universities took control of the halls. In Oxford about sixty came thus under University jurisdiction in the 1480's. At that time there were ten colleges, but the college system was destined to eliminate nearly all the halls. The obvious advantages of collegiate organization, at least from the University's standpoint, and a policy of allowing and finally of requiring undergraduates to live in colleges ended the need for hostels. The earliest colleges, however, were intended for graduates, not undergraduates.

The statutes of Merton, Oxford, were the model for those of Peterhouse, the oldest of Cambridge colleges, and for other early colleges in both universities. Christ Church, Oxford, begun by Wolsey and completed by Henry VIII, had no statutes at all and was governed by a dean and a chapter of canons. All other colleges were governed by a head and a body of Fellows. The Provost of King's and the Master of Trinity, Cambridge, were appointed by the Crown; the Master of Magdalene, Cambridge, by heirs of the founder. In most colleges the head was elected by the Fellows from their own ranks. Fellows of Emmanuel, if they did not choose one of themselves, were supposed to give preference to a member of Christ's; similarly Fellows of Sidney Sussex to a member of Trinity. One Elizabethan Master, James Pilkington of St. John's, Cambridge, who resigned in 1561 to become Bishop of Durham, was succeeded by his brother. On occasion the Crown interfered with elections by recommending a favorite; sometimes with happy results, as when a royal intimation inspired the Fellows of Corpus Christi to elect Matthew Parker in 1544. In the sixteenth century and for a long time afterward all the heads were divines. Early statutes often stipulated that the Master be a B.D. or D.D. or, at the very least, an M.A. studying Theology.

Bishop Pilkington wrote to Cecil in 1561 that, as for the heads of Cambridge colleges, "some be such that I cannot tell whether they do less harm being absent or present, and none or very few do any good." This opinion from a man who had until recently been a Master himself sprang partly from religious quarrels of the day but may also reflect something of that weary cynicism in which harried academic administrators find final relief. Tudor Masters were of all kinds. Thomas Fuller's delineation, in his *Holy State* (1642), of "the good master of a college" portrays one whose learning "if beneath eminency is far above contempt," who "not only keeps the statutes in his study but observes them," "disdains to nourish dissension amongst the members of his house," and "in his elections he

30

Christ Church, Oxford. Founded by Cardinal Wolsey in 1518 as Cardinal College and planned on a magnificent scale. It was completed by King Henry VIII. (From David Loggan, *Oxonia Illustrata*, 1675.)

respecteth merit." There were also slippery timeservers like Andrew Perne of Peterhouse, notorious for his alacrity in adjusting his religion to the prevalent official doctrines. There were difficult characters like Degory Nichols of Magdalene, who annoyed the Fellows by letting his cows graze in the college court. Some heads were constantly at odds with the Fellows. Dr. Caius of Gonville and Caius punished certain Fellows by putting them in stocks. At one time or another he expelled twenty Fellows from his unruly college. None of the numerous Elizabethan quarrels between Master and Fellows equaled the famous thirty years' war between Richard Bentley and the Fellows of Trinity, Cambridge, in the eighteenth century, but Elizabethan Cambridge witnessed extensive feuds, some of which demanded the combined efforts of Government and Chancellor to end.

Fellows, like Masters, included all the familiar academic types: distinguished scholars, sober divines, conscientious tutors, and on the other hand some whose distinction is not easy to discover. Tudor Fellows do not seem to have been excessively sociable, but perhaps amiability was not considered the highest of academic virtues. They displayed the sensitivity to criticism, zeal for protecting their rights, devotion to principle, and talent for intrigue often found in members of learned societies. Gabriel Harvey of Pembroke, Cambridge, with his grumbling and his genius for making enemies—two other Pembroke Fellows voted against his M.A. degree—may have been more difficult than most, but his very combination of studiousness and irritability renders him an authentic academic type.

Tutors were drawn from Fellows, of course. Medieval Fellows, in the days before the tutorial system, had no teaching duties. Some statutes required or permitted a certain number of Fellows to study law or medicine, but in Tudor as well as in medieval universities most Fellows were in the Faculty of Theology. The number of Fellows at Cambridge increased by a third between 1564 and 1573—there were 320 in 1573—and most of those elected appear to have been in their early twenties. As Regent Masters they held the balance of power in the

University; as young men in a hurry, many of them with forth-right opinions on ecclesiastical questions, they sometimes seemed obstreperous to their elders. The new statutes of 1570, drawn up principally by Whitgift, deprived them of their power.

Fellowships, as everyone understood, had to be surrendered if the holders married, but not everyone agreed on how long unmarried Fellows should keep their appointments. Tradition-ally they had been expected to leave after finishing advanced studies. If they stayed on, as in Elizabethan times became increasingly common, they did not profit the Church. At least this seems to have been the view of the bishops, who in 1584 opposed Puritan suggestions that some Fellows remain in the University. Emmanuel's statutes warn that Fellows must not regard the college as "a perpetual abode." Notwithstanding this explicitness, the Crown nullified the statute. Fellowships came to be looked upon as lifetime appointments or ones to which re-election from time to time was a formality. For a long time there was even a custom of buying and selling fellowships. This abuse required Parliamentary action (1575, 1589) to correct.

"Every college is a little commonwealth in itself," wrote a seventeenth-century Chancellor of Cambridge. Like larger commonwealths, these had constitutional problems and finan-cial crises. Colleges lived off income from their endowments, but as landlords dependent on fixed revenues they suffered from monetary inflation, bad harvests, and other economic woes. They had adopted a practice of granting long leases at low rentals but exacting heavy "fines," payments customarily made when leases were granted or renewed. Parliament in 1571 and 1576 forbade such long leases but decreed (1576) that in all new leases not less than one third of the rent should be paid in grain valued at a price stipulated by the Act; or, in lieu of grain, in money equal to the current market price. This legis-lation assured colleges of cheap bread if the rent was paid in grain, for the producer's price was fixed and he could not raise it. If he paid in cash, the colleges were assured of more revenue

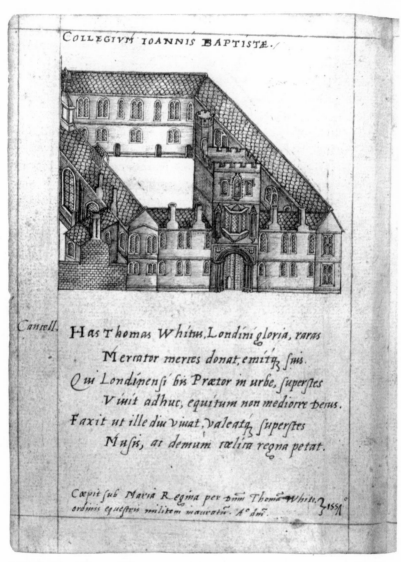

St. John's College, Oxford. Founded in 1555 by Sir Thomas White, a London merchant. This drawing is one of a series made by John Bereblock, an Oxford graduate, in 1566. (Courtesy of the Bodleian Library, Oxford.)

whenever market prices rose. In time this third provided far more income than did the other two thirds and enabled the colleges to grant allowances to Fellows or to increase existing allowances.

Undergraduates were scholars, commoners, or pensioners. In the language of statutes, "scholar" signified a student who, like the graduate Fellows, was "on the foundation," that is, had "exhibitions" or grants or scholarships and received his food and lodging from college funds. Statutes of many colleges specified that a number of commoners and pensioners could or should be received. These were members of a college who were not "on the foundation" and did not always live in college. The name "commoner" implied no invidious social distinctions but merely differentiated students not on the foundation from others. Often the fellow commoners, as they were called, were noble or wealthy youths. "Pensioners," though the term may be of later date than "commoner," had the same relation to a college. Roger Ascham complains in the late 1540's about rich commoners or pensioners who come to the university without serious intellectual purpose and distract the more sober sort. Fellow commoners dined with the Fellows and, if nobles, had enviable privileges, including the convenient one of getting degrees without completing the ordinary requirements. But they were not likely to need or desire degrees. At the opposite extreme were poor students of the kind called "sizars" at Cambridge; menials who performed lowly tasks and ate the leavings from their betters' tables.

Oxford is thought to have had a thousand students at most in 1450. It conferred fewer than a hundred degrees a year. At its low point in the sixteenth century, 1542–1548, it granted only 173 B.A. degrees in six years, according to one account. Cambridge granted 191 B.A. degrees in the same period. In Mary's reign and the early years of Elizabeth's, sixty to seventy men a year supplicated for degrees at Oxford. Cambridge granted only ninety M.A. and 167 B.A. degrees in 1549–1553; in 1557–1558 the totals were 125 and 195. In 1559 only twenty-eight men took the B.A. degree there. William Harrison's description of the universities (1577) says there were about 3,000 students "in them both." During most of the Elizabethan reign Cambridge was the larger. In 1564 it had 1,267 resident members in colleges; in 1569, 1,630; by the end of the century, almost 2,000. In 1560 it gave sixty B.A. degrees; in 1570, 114; in 1583, 277, the largest number in any year of that century. Oxford graduated 157 in the same year. Oxford averaged 270 matriculates annually in 1593–1603. Cambridge in 1597 reported 1,950 students in the colleges and in addition 657 "graduates" (in residence, presumably) and 122 preachers, these last "almost all unprovided for."

Students entered the university as young as twelve, but it is safe to say that the average entering age in the sixteenth century was fifteen, a year higher in the following century. Medieval statutes assumed that freshmen would be fourteen, and the 1570 code for Cambridge ordered that no scholar be admitted unless he had completed his fourteenth year.

Students were bound to be in residence three terms a year (October to Christmas, January to Easter, Easter to July), and some stayed on during the long vacation. They had brief respites after each term and sometimes unscheduled ones when plague broke out. Discipline was naturally paternalistic, partly because of the very youthfulness of undergraduates, partly because of the clerical and semimonastic traditions of the older colleges and the general severity of discipline in medieval and Tudor life. University officers invariably complained that students were going to the dogs, and indeed Elizabethan undergraduates had a reputation for incorrigible unruliness and insubordination. Adults, men twenty years old or over, were formally rebuked, fined, imprisoned, or in extreme cases expelled for delinquencies. For undergraduate malefactors the standard punishment was flogging.

Medieval and Renaissance universities had no official interest in sports or games and assumed no responsibility for amusing undergraduates; paternalism of this kind is an American eccentricity. Statutes strictly forbade most of the recreations naturally attractive to young men, yet the monotonous regularity of these

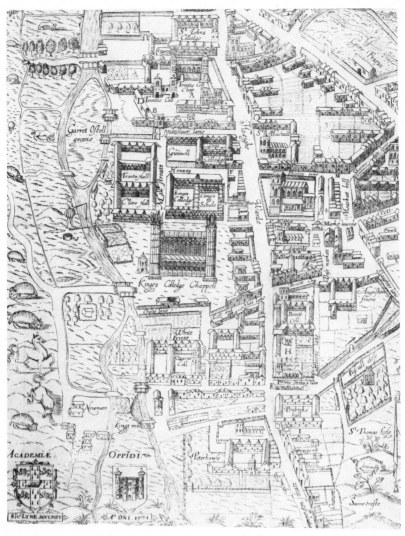

Elizabethan Cambridge. This is part of an engraving by Richard Lyne, 1574, for insertion in John Caius' *Historiae Cantabrigiensis Academiae,* 1574. (Folger Shakespeare Library.)

prohibitions proves that they were honored in the breach as well as the observance. Again and again it was necessary to forbid gambling and possession of arms, birds, cards, and hounds. Tobacco was deplored and forbidden. A special object of official displeasure was addiction to silks and fine array. Academic officers seem to have been obsessed by this evil. Oversize ruffs and the wearing of swords and of silks or velvets, unless one's social rank clearly justified this, were specifically forbidden. Even bathing was frowned upon. A decree of the Vice-Chancellor and heads of colleges at Cambridge in 1571, "That No One Go Into the Water," forbade students to enter any river or pond within the county of Cambridge, "either for swimming or bathing, whether by day or by night," on penalty of being severely whipped in the college hall. One of the few forms of exercise condoned was walking, but older statutes stipulated that this was to be done in pairs, never alone. Dr. Caius' statutes (1572) for his college contained the usual prohibitions of idle or corrupting pastimes but were licentious enough to tolerate ball-catching *(pilae reciprocatio)*.

A higher form of entertainment was furnished occasionally by student performances of Greek, Latin, or English plays in college halls. Christ Church, Oxford, appears to have had in its early years two Latin and Greek tragedies and two comedies each year. Sometimes university plays were good enough to achieve a place in literary history. Such, for instance, were the three *Parnassus* plays, English comedies presented at St. John's, Cambridge, 1598–1601. A Cambridge Latin comedy, *Ignoramus*, which was acted before King James and gave him much pleasure, became an academic classic. The supreme English dramatist, Shakespeare, attended neither university, but his Hamlet is the most famous university student in English drama. The title-page of the first quarto edition of *Hamlet* (1603) says that the play was acted "in the two universities of Cambridge and Oxford," but this must mean in the town, not in the college halls. Touring companies succeeded, legally or illegally, in giving performances in the towns, but university authorities were strongly and consistently hostile to such entertainment and

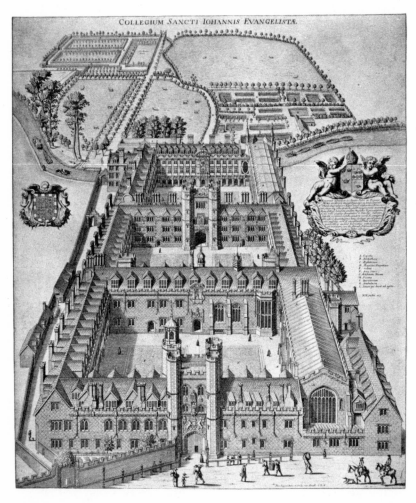

St. John's College, Cambridge. Like Christ's, this college was founded
(1511) by Lady Margaret Beaufort with the advice of Bishop Fisher.
(From David Loggan, *Cantabrigia Illustrata*, 1676–1690.)

objected repeatedly to plays and players in the neighborhood.

Extramural dissipation not only endangered morals but often provoked fighting between students and townsmen. "The relation of the University to the city," as a writer on Elizabethan Oxford observes, "was necessarily antagonistic." Inherent economic and legal conflicts of interest in university towns perpetuated animosities between local residents, especially tradesmen, and members of the university and led to suits, appeals to Government, and disorder. William Harrison, taking the usual academic view, asserts (1577) that the townsmen "are glad when they match and annoy the students by encroaching on their liberties and keep them bare by extreme sale of their wares." No doubt, but the townsmen for their part resented the arrogance and contempt with which they were treated (so they said) by members of the university.

Students kept early hours. Four o'clock was a common hour for rising in the sixteenth century. College gates closed at eight P.M. in winter, nine in summer. That living was uncomfortable by our standards goes without saying. Lecture halls were unheated. Even in college halls or rooms fires were a luxury. In a sermon preached in 1550 a Cambridge divine describes how the scholars there study at night until nine or ten "and then being without fire are fain to walk or run up and down half an hour, to get a heat in their feet when they go to bed." Poor scholars were not so badly off as their medieval predecessors, who begged for a living, but they had a hard enough time. (Oxford, defending itself in 1460 against a charge by friars that fees were too high, indignantly denied that degrees were cheaper at Cambridge.) Fees were paid directly to tutors and lecturers, but there were also miscellaneous charges by university officers that had to be met.

We have noted the active role of Government in academic affairs. Once or twice in a reign royalty itself condescended to visit the universities. Henry VII, accompanied by his mother and his son, Prince Henry, stopped at Cambridge in 1506 on his way to the shrine of St. Mary of Walsingham. Elizabeth paid a visit to Cambridge in 1564 and to Oxford in 1566 and 1592.

James visited Oxford in 1605 and 1614, Cambridge twice in 1615 and again in 1624. For these visits proud but anxious university officers made exhaustive preparations. We have interesting documents describing the plans for Elizabeth's visits to Oxford and equally interesting contemporary accounts of what happened on those visits. The Queen was treated to an interminable round of Greek and Latin greetings, orations, sermons, verses, and plays. Disputations were presented on such edifying topics as "Whether the glory of the blessed will be equal," "Whether air changes bodies more than food and drink do," "Whether astrologers should be banished from the commonwealth." How she endured them all we can only guess. We do know how thoroughly James I, who esteemed himself as a theologian and philosopher, enjoyed a celebrated disputation in Cambridge in 1615. He even intervened in it.

William Harrison, who owed allegiance to both universities, praised Oxford for its larger streets and thought that "for curious workmanship and private commodities" the colleges there were "much more stately, magnificent, and commodious than those of Cambridge." But for "uniformity of building, orderly compaction, and politic regiment," the town of Cambridge exceeded Oxford "many, many a fold." King's College Chapel at Cambridge and the Divinity School at Oxford he considered two of the most beautiful buildings in Europe. "In all other things there is so great equality between these two universities as no man can imagine how to set down any greater, so that they seem to be the body of one well-ordered commonwealth, only divided by distance of place and not in friendly consent and orders." We cannot do better than to accept this judicious Elizabethan appraisal. Other graduates, Francis Bacon among them, could be more critical. But the final word belongs to Chief Justice Coke, Bacon's lifelong rival and, like him, an alumnus of Trinity, Cambridge. The universities of Oxford and Cambridge, wrote Coke, were "the suns, eyes, and minds of the kingdom, from which religion, liberal education, and sound learning are spread most abundantly to every part of the realm."

Elizabethan Oxford. Engraved by Augustine Ryther, 1588, after Ralph
the only one

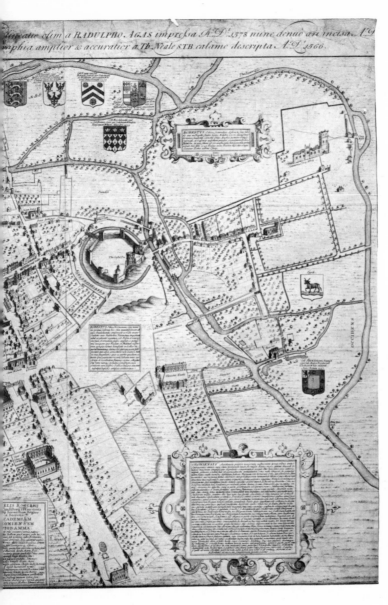

as' drawing of 1578. This Folger copy is one of two known and
damaged.

SUGGESTED READING

Since Oxford and Cambridge were medieval foundations, the best introduction to their Tudor history is made through acquaintance with the nature of medieval universities. This can be obtained from C. H. Haskins, *The Rise of Universities* (Ithaca, 1957), the best short introduction, and from the longer work by Hastings Rashdall, *The Universities of Europe in the Middle Ages,* ed. F. M. Powicke and A. B. Emden (Oxford, 1936). *University Records and Life in the Middle Ages,* ed. Lynn Thorndike (New York, 1944), is a convenient collection of documents, in translation, from and about Continental universities.

Oxford statutes to 1634 are collected in *Statuta Antiqua Universitatis Oxoniensis,* ed. Strickland Gibson (Oxford, 1931). Many valuable works on Oxford history are published in the volumes issued by the Oxford Historical Society; for example, *Elizabethan Oxford,* ed. Charles Plummer (1887); *Epistolae Academicae Oxonienses,* ed H. Anstey (1898); and *Register of the University of Oxford,* vol. II, 1571–1622, pt. 1, Introduction, ed. Andrew Clark (1887), an indispensable work. Anthony Wood's famous *History of the Antiquities of the University of Oxford* first appeared in Latin (1674; English version, 1791–1796). His *Athenae Oxonienses* (1691–1692) is a series of brief biographies of distinguished men educated at Oxford between 1500 and 1690. The standard modern history is that of C. E. Mallet, *A History of the University of Oxford* (London, 1924–1927).

For Cambridge documents see James Heywood (ed.), *Collection of Statutes for the University and Colleges of Cambridge* (London, 1840); George Peacock, *Observations on the Statutes of the University of Cambridge* (London, 1841); James Heywood and Thomas Wright, (eds.), *Cambridge University Transactions During the Puritan Controversies of the 16th and 17th Centuries* (London, 1854). On fifteenth-century Cambridge there is useful information in S. M. Leathes' introduction to *Grace Book A* (Cambridge, 1897); he prints also a Cambridge diary for 1533–1534. Older chronicles of the University were superseded by the writings of C. H. Cooper:

Annals of Cambridge (Cambridge, 1842–1853), *Memorials of Cambridge* (Cambridge, 1858–1866), *Athenae Cantabrigienses* (Cambridge, 1858–1861). For general history of the University there is a three-volume work, *The University of Cambridge,* by J. B. Mullinger (Cambridge, 1873–1888), and a one-volume condensation of this by the same author (London, 1888). W. W. Rouse Ball, *Cambridge Papers* (Cambridge, 1918), includes essays on the Tudor and Stuart periods. Two of the most useful books on Cambridge are also among the most recent. H. C. Porter, *Reformation and Reaction in Tudor Cambridge* (Cambridge, 1958), treats of the place of the University in the ecclesiastical history of the times. William T. Costello, *The Scholastic Curriculum at Early Seventeenth-Century Cambridge* (Cambridge, Mass., 1958), describes disputations and other academic exercises. Both books use unprinted documents from the University and college archives. Another important study, *Oxford and Cambridge in Transition, 1558–1642,* by Mark H. Curtis, is in press.

Published histories of the various colleges in each university are too numerous to list here. They differ a good deal in scope and merit but are always worth consulting.

William Harrison's account of the universities, first published in Holinshed's *Chronicles* (1577), was reprinted by L. Withington (London, ca. 1902). *College Life in the Times of James the First* contains the diary of Simonds d'Ewes. An unpublished set of "directions for a Student in the University," by Richard Holdsworth, d'Ewes' tutor at Cambridge, is quoted by Costello. J. A. Venn, *Early Collegiate Life* (Cambridge, 1913), has material on the sixteenth and seventeenth centuries. The *Parnassus* plays were edited by J. B. Leishman (London, 1949).

Useful studies of special topics will be found in E. G. Rupp, *Studies in the Making of the English Protestant Tradition* (Cambridge, 1947); M. M. Knappen, *Tudor Puritanism* (Chicago, 1939); William Haller, *The Rise of Puritanism* (New York, 1938); C. H. Garrett, *The Marian Exiles* (Cambridge, 1938); *Shakespeare's England* (Oxford, 1916); Louis B. Wright, *Middle-Class Culture in Elizabethan England* (Ithaca, 1958); J. E. Sandys, *A History of Classical Scholarship* (Cambridge, 1903–1908); F. S. Boas, *University Drama in the Tudor Age* (Oxford, 1914) and *Shakespeare and the Universities* (London, 1922); P. S. Allen, *Erasmus* (Oxford, 1934).